Bakary and the River

poems by

Clifford Bernier

Finishing Line Press
Georgetown, Kentucky

Bakary
and the River

Copyright © 2025 by Clifford Bernier
ISBN 979-8-89990-110-2 First Edition
All rights reserved under International and Pan-American Copyright Conventions. No part of this book may be reproduced in any manner whatsoever without written permission from the publisher, except in the case of brief quotations embodied in critical articles and reviews.

Publisher: Leah Huete de Maines
Editor: Christen Kincaid
Cover Art: Clifford Bernier
Author Photo: Clifford Bernier
Cover Design: Elizabeth Maines McCleavy

Order online: www.finishinglinepress.com
also available on amazon.com

Author inquiries and mail orders:
Finishing Line Press
PO Box 1626
Georgetown, Kentucky 40324
USA

Contents

Memory 1
Rivertrail 2
Batteau 3
Riverman 5
Bakary 6
Running Creek 7
Wildlife Refuge 8
Peace 9
Confluence 10
Fire 11
Fire Too 12
End of the Water 13
Tauxemont 14
Accotink 16
Conflux 17
Headwater 18
Chesapeack 19
Solomon 20
Cuyahoga 22
Detroit 23
Wabash 24
St. Louis 25
Mississippi 26
Messippi 27
Mississippi Too 28
Mississippi Blues 29
Ohio 30
Colonial Beach 31

Rappahannock 32
Pamunkey 34
Powhatan 35
First Landing 37

For my family. All the light I need.

Memory

Along the creek that leads to the
river sheet moss and shield fern
creep with red oak and hickory
and the leaping of bass in the rain.
Yellowthroat summon the eagle
and vireo summon the osprey.
The riverbird knows rain brings
mice and bugs and frying pans
of fish like the foraging settlers
saw and fantasies flying above
the crossing at Powell's Creek
and the Powhatan and the James,
above thought and the reach of
history along the lives of survivors,
natives who loved the land
and invaders who burned it,
paddling languidly along the pines
and the blueback in the drizzle,
gone now except for cicadas
and the plink of green arrow
and the splash of alewives and
sturgeon and soaring memory.

Rivertrail

Smell of wet grass by the beaverpond,
banter of birds in the bushes. The river
knows its loping leads to the sea. But
still it lopes. As do we. Bakary and I,
I and I, cool runnings as branches bend
and breezes bray. Current carries us,
by Green Hill, by Dixon Landing, Tye River
Overlook. By black bears and batteaux.
Hogheads of tobacco, wheat, corn, hens—
Boatmen helming the waterways for
commerce and crops like the elusive
river, never the same twice since Heraclitus
and butterflies. Cargo of venison and
fruit. You load the nut, the berry, the
drupe. The pecan, the beet, the bean.
And pole the craft to market through the
rapids by the rivertrail,

push from shore and steer the boat to sea.

Batteau

Over the valley a river runs
like a splash of stars on a
summer night. Bakary and I
shoot the rapids—the swan,
the dolphin, dragon's eye—
load our sweet cargo and
ride the current to Richmond.
We have seen the river rage
like Orion, grieve like Cygnus,
wine like Aquila, keep bears.
By the foxtail the tide crawls
like a cottonmouth—Bakary
steers the batteau to a cove
and grills rabbit. Hogheads
of tobacco earn our wages—
peas, wheat, goat, squash
bring profit. On the far bank
villagers hawk their harvest—
grapes, sunflower, beans—
nereids, nymphs, scorpions
guide our riverboat drifting
through Cepheus and Lyra
to markets downriver. Whose
truth navigates the flow—
the Okee, the Great Hare,
the Sun, the Wind, Ahone—
canoes and ferries, freighters,
Monacans, Saponi, Nottoway—
merchants serpent-bit as
Earth caught fire and Sky was
sliced by the sickle of time.
We pole away from the shore—
from the real and true and
known and unknown to a
fantasy of adventure along
the river Bakary plies
with our sweet cargo tossed
like a splash of stars trading

corn and creed for Polaris
and Phaethon's bones and
possum and Andromeda saved.

Riverman

Bakary pilots through Perseus
while I prepare goods for purchase.
The glow of Cassiopeia mingles
with the fires of Monahassanaugh,
which ignores us. The mosquitos
don't, however, nor do the packet
boats and their passengers,
genteel from Lynchburg with their
top hats, petticoats and Orinoco
dreams for purveyors in Richmond.
Bandits on the river rival the rapids,
Helios burns like Prometheus
and I have become the river,
resonant with light from the foam,
a deep and amniotic rush
on the rustling bank by Rassawek,
dodging ferries and fishing lines,
dugout canoes tied to shore,
evening cooking ruffled by smoke,
trading a language I do not know
for a night of stories from the stars,
not my stars, not my stories
still the wheel of Arcturus circling
like a bear, guiding our chariot
by Mowhemcho where Bakary
bridles Pegasus and smiles back at me—

a riverman.

Bakary

Bakary says he's a Batteauman
and I don't mind. Batteaux
run tobacco from Lynchburg
to Richmond for market, barter
produce and livestock with settlers
who contract their strength and
skill to command the rapids and
rustlers on their return. He's the
best. Unbothered by the unknown,
unknown by the unbothered,
I rib he's the striped bass on the
gunwale, the brook trout on the
barby. Along the rivercreek we
grab frogs and grill legs French-style,
with haricots verts and a red.
Like the Gambia in the Gambia,
he says. He would be Antares,
or the seventh labor of Hercules,
or Odysseus back from the dead.
Or a hero I have not understood.
Underneath the current, in the
underworld, chokers scrape
for scraps and eels slither
like snakes. Chattel upriver clear
quarters for corn, wheat, cows.
So the owner and the overseer—
so Bakary, the Gambian, the slave.

Running Creek

The Running Creek is almost dry.
Little rain these languid months.
A trickle through rocks is all.
Ferns and moss feed the bank
while birds chatter like naiads or
Cygnus chanting *the beautiful boy.*
Is this where it begins—the slow
transformation of rain to creek
to stream to river—Medusa's
snakes and the dragon rising—
Bakary poling against the tide
for the journey back to the real—
the planting and the picking
and the clearing and the building—
where drumming and trilling
are truer than the stony silence
of the immeasurable river
and the Running Creek in draught.

Wildlife Refuge

These pines like sentinels of the past—
past the turkey, the pheasant, the starling,
the Union troops turned toward Petersburg
crossing the James at Powell's Creek,
bodies stacked like firewood
burnt in managed clearing in this refuge.
Like Hill's raftered bones at Logres
silent in remembrance in legend
though no marker among the loblolly
only the bluejay and the cardinal
and the long cry of the American crow.

Peace

Peace like the Appomattox
in the birdcall and arrow arum
flowing gently to the James.
Fish flop and flies flip. The
Powhatan had been here. The
invaders brought war. But
the river remains, quiet in the
afterward sun—the current is flat,
the river refracts like a mirror,
muskets laid down in peace,
my stool perched on this jetty
out of words, out of time.

Confluence

At the confluence of the James
and the Tye—or Tiber—the Friar,
the Priest, and Cardinal peaks
overlook rolling hills of laurel
and hemlock. Mist blurs the valley
where farmland is planted in rows.
The James ran backward in '69
propelled by hurricane winds
as a man stepped on the moon
and the Trinity receded into
Aquarius and bell bottoms and
a fiction no one could construct.
Tiber flooded as Rome burned
and the Tye ran forward again,
ancient gods dimmed in the haze,
smoke from fires in Canada now
as the known world burned anew,
the Religious Range shrouded,
the confluence still as a mirror,
the crops in the valley plentiful
and green in deep rows growing tall.

Fire

The fires on the bank
have their purpose—
cooking or signaling
or warmth or friendship—
says Bakary as we
slide by Massinacak
under sparkling Lyra.
But another as well—
comfort that life will end
like the logs in the flame
and its hardships and
mysteries will fade
like smoke released to
the wind and stars
and the glittering embers
that guide the night sky.

Fire Too

That's not how I see it, I say,
cruising through Corona Borealis,
fires show what is beyond
the logs and smoke and flame
and tell of a time after time
that is full and warm and pure
and true and the unspoken hope
of our deepest unseen longing.

Indeed, says Bakary.

End of the Water

At the End of the Water
that flows to the Trader
only the lapping of
driftwood interrupts
the dialog of cardinal
and crow and the
Doeg who lived here
with mink and maize
and dugout canoes
when John Smith
sailed in with settlers
and disease that
pushed the tribes
westward leaving
trails and techniques
and villages with
pleasure boats
tied to docks that
interrupt the bay
with engines
and wakes from
Quantico and Route 1
traffic rushing upriver
past Occoquan along
the ancient Potomac Path.

Tauxemont

As I rounded the point
Where the Water Ends
a dugout paddled
toward me speaking
Algonquian I guessed
from the Tauxenent
tribe along the Place
Where People Trade.
Powhatan would
betray me but the Taux
offered a feast. Did
they know I was raised
in Tauxemont, on a
horseshoe gravel road
in the '60s—potluck
dinners and open doors
and nature camp at the
nursery school—
Patawomeck slipping
nearby into marshes
and tributaries and
villages of warriors
and shamans planting
corn and beans, fishing
perch and carp in the
long stream while fighting
Sioux and Iroquois
and the meager harvest
of fallow soil—
Would I, Jonas Profit,
fisherman and sailor,
John Smith's crewman,
join the werowance for
supper—bear, deer, quail,
squash—fellowship and
trade and understanding—
Yes! My car for a canoe,
my house for a hut,
my tales of the wandering

world for the call of
catching turtle and newt
and crayfish again in the
creek in the woods behind
the camp running
down with bare feet on
the unrelenting gravel of
Tauxenent—no—
Tauxemont Road.

Accotink

On the barge we were fourteen—
bare crew for an expedition but
sufficient—doctor, tailor, carpenter,
blacksmith—charged with mapping
the Chesapeack and tribes and rumors
of glistering pin-dust on rocks above
mighty falls—Moyumpse, Mattaponi,
Chickahominy, Manahoac, Pamunkey—
names with corn to trade for swords,
beads, hens, muskets, grindstone.
Raptors swooped and carp jumped
as our shallop parsed the waters of
the very merry and the playful one—
the Piankatank, the Rappahannock,
Patawomek, Patuxent—fertile with
fox and deer and badger before the
draught and the burning and betrayal
and the starving time—all true while
I, Richard Keale, fish merchant of the
Discovery, alone knew the plentiful
swimmers lifting their heads above the
spangling surf, and which were edible.

Conflux

Where the Cowpasture meets the Jackson
whitewater ripples by a low island
green with sycamore and chestnut and
the call of goldfinch and indigo bunting.
The Cowpasture is placid as the fields
below the Allegheny that feed livestock
still as mountains in the lingering sun.
The James starts here. Or rather, your
awareness starts here. In the reeds, the
roots, the recognition of the endless
in the realization of the rapids, the chatter
of cricket and cardinal, buzz of dragonfly
and breeze—mind mingling with the
motion and the senses in the conflux
of relation and being, sweet gum and
peregrine perched on the bank. Trout
know you, bass look through you to the
raccoon and possum above the leaping
plume and lilting river, the limitless
headwater, unending origin, sourceless source.

Headwater

Above the headwater of the James
the white tails of rapids and deer
engage the warbler and wren and
the rooster crowing in the barn by
the field where hay is piled in
Stevens' mows and islands part
like Walcott's star-apple kingdom
between ridges of rainbow rock
and the storied Devil's Backbone.
The rockfish seeing through me
sees the squirrel seeing through
the grouse seeing through the skunk
seeing through the poplar near
Iron Gate. Arrowwood tells the elm
I am the source but the birch tells
the pawpaw it is I and the stream
says the rain and the rivulet says
the sea. While Cassiopeia betrays
Andromeda and Wynken is tossed
in a flood of light. The James is a
flower between two rivers in the
ear-of-wheat star says the croaker
to the woodchuck as the doe
becomes a donkey and the elk
becomes a chub, seeing through the
hogsuckers and bullheads, the red
horse and herring, speaking through
me as through the badgers and sassafras
and skimmers and weasels and goats.

Chesapeack

From the boardwalk I see the
Discovery barge row upstream.
The Chesapeack is as wide as
the ocean here, and the rising
sun spangles the crossing like
bracelets of coral. Its travel
maps the bay and the rivers,
the wildlife and woods, nations
and ways of the unknown.
The priest in bear skin and
wolf teeth, the shaman in
skull shawl and snake tail,
the squaw in paint and beads.
Dream compels the voyage
from the Mermaid Tavern
where Anas Todkill meets
Master Shakespeare in a
fantasy of history, Prospero
shipwrecked on Devill's
Isle, storm clouds swinging
from the south, beachgoers
retreating to resorts. Miranda
wooed and Pokahontas
purchased for a copper kettle.
Sorcerers toss tobacco and seed
to pacify the dark god, tempest
of thunder and lightning
unseen in London or Milan—
Massawomekes warring with
Pattawomekes as English with
Turks and Antonio with his
brother. From pie and sack to
drum and mash. Two months on
oysters and roots as the rain
recedes, Ariel is freed and a gull
settles on the pier by the crab
house, light finishes the day and
I stand on *Discovery's* prow
by the lifting waves like white feathers.

Solomon

Osprey call to the robin
and mockingbird at land's
end on Solomon's Island,
Chesapeack glistening like
gold rumored in the rapids
at Little Falls. Fishing pier
long in the bay, oyster
cannery long gone, willow
weeping like the horizon
under the ever-rising sun.
At the Tiki Bar King Solomon
entertains 700 wives in silk
and camphor with wine and
spirit, though he will recall
their love more than wine—
wisdom passed in proverb—
as wynde whirls the Southern
Isles and Propero's magic
heals lovers and fiends—
madness and folly and sorrow
knowledge's only gain—
schooners and sloops and
bugeyes moored on the docks
for the distant storm,
Bourne on the skipjack *Discovery*
with us along the Patuxent
as gusts rip the mast and sail
and we maroon in Limbo,
among uninhabited shores
yet not with the hens and
turkies of Bermooth but the
bluefish, drum, and flounder
of Solomon. *Be like a young roe
or hart upon the mountain of spices*
he sings as we explore cypress
for a northwest passage and
seagulls swoop past shoals
like flocks of shipwrecked sheep.
All the rivers run to the sea yet

the sea is not full he preaches,
300 concubines in rubies and
myrrh by his sceptre swigging
aquavitae as the mockingbird
repeats the metaphor and the
bay returns to the river mystic
and sourceless as the turning
season of oyster and pomegranate
under the ancient sun glistening with pearls.

Cuyahoga

The Cuyahoga flat as the cornfields
that approach the city, crooked at
the bend to Irishtown and the Great
Water, ore weighting freighters for the
steel mills and mining of Cleveland.
On the cliffs above the river the old
factories recall the fire, the whiskey,
the shanties by the docks and skiffs,
the dark hills a long way from the
green bogs of the potatoless island
of famine and poets and Fergus.
At Settlers Landing, an ampitheater
sits by the crane that lifted coal,
driftlogs and ducks float by a fountain,
and the riverboat tied to the pier
prepares to ferry loaders and landlubbers
by the revelry and rusting shipworks

of the Flats.

Detroit

The Detroit at night settles
the lights of Windsor like
fur traded by the Ottawa
with French before the war.
Ezekial Solomon settled
Jews—Abraham leading
from exile to the Union
and roots for cloth, muskets
and metal in the strait of
Great Water and New France.
By the lighthouse the
Renaissance Center
towers above—Chrysler
and Cadillac merged with
Mi'kmaq and Huron on
the hunting ground of the
Chippewa and Shawnee
and the wisdom of Solomon
in the welcoming Detroit
and the warm lights of Windsor.

Wabash

At the Place of Peace
that shines white
buffalo fish jump for
bugs and goldfinch
sing in the hickory.
Mink and heron mix
with otter and owl
on the bluff, islands
of stone and jewel
weed part the current
as Prophetstown
burns. He is Moses
Harrison says as
Shawnee retreat and
the Wabash drains
Indiana like a letting
over limestone and
Tecumseh's confederacy
from the confluence
to the White and Ohio
wavy like the flickering
river and the prophet
and the shifting promise

of peace.

St. Louis

Bakary dreams of rivers.
The Cuyahoga's crooked jaw
and the Wabash pure over white
stones. The Mississippi thick as
honey. Barges and steamboats,
flatboats and yawls—Jim and the
wigwam as Huck's raft slides by
the mystical lights of St. Louis
free as the fleeing current,
fleeting as the hope of release—
slave to the widow and race,
yes'm and sho'nuff and the dogs
in pursuit through the strawberry
and cottonwood to Jackson Island—
Jackson washing into the James
like the Tippecanoe into Wabash—
the Missouri into the Mississippi—
Mississippi into the Ohio—
metaphor on metaphor under the
stars that just happened, Osage
trading hides for guns and land,
Spanish for *criollo* and gumbo,
French *habitants* founding a city,
enslaved yet free to marry,
multicultural post of rapscallions
lamplit like Sollermun's wives,
Sacagawea and Pokahantas and
I and I on the *Discovery* floating
downstream by draggers and
witches and whitecaps and sloughs
to land's end and snakeskins
and towheads and Cairo and freedom.

Mississippi

On the muddy bank the
Mississippi dangles like
honey locust or summer
grape or bluestem grass
tangled with amaranth
and ragweed. Sparrows
play the jig of the tide
against the drift and the
passage of shadows.
By a movement of song
with a blackbird, red
wings tripping the sun,
cypress plucked in time,
intro to a piece without
coda, to a river without end.

Messippi

The long flow of time. From
the cave cool for the grain
and shelter to the bottomland
fishing and hunting to the
barges and steamers the
Obijwe and Osage and Omaha
saw scrape the Great River
until trains lengthened the flow
and the land became property
and the mountain became ore
and the Mother of Rivers lost
her umbilical cord to the
surgeon and the steeple and the bell.

Mississippi Too

Yet the river rolls on.
Indifferent to victor or
vanquished, unafraid
of hail or heat, impartial
to action or idea. Only
the rustle of sage and
sumac, splish and
ripple of wake on the
bank, ramble of breeze
in the bristlegrass.
Snappers and bugs
buzz the rough, coyote
and ferret prowl the
prairie. Pawnees and
Poncas and mounds
and pelts and tugs
and tows and hobos.
Administrations and wars.
The call of the cardinal.
And the imperishable run

of the current.

Mississippi Blues

I sat on a log
by the Mississippi
and listened to
the blues. It's voice
rose from the
shoals and mingled
with the burr and
the buckeye. It
sang of deckhands
and warriors, slavers
and runaways,
freemen and
rogues. Tenders
overturned and
packets swept under.
Rusted hulls up
and keels broken
by longing. A dredge
cleared the channel
and the fallacies of
fortune, the rich,
the castoff, the
cruel and the kind,
the just and the
wronged. Each
sluicing downstream
or sunk to silt. And
the blues was the
breeze and the
breeze was the river
and the river was
the lost and the
lost was the driftwood
and detritus tramping
anew over the alluvial plain.

Ohio

The Allegheny and the
Monongahela feed the
Ohio as Bakary and
Jim paddle North
from Cairo to the
free states, join the
Black Brigade in Cincy
and the Underground
Railroad with the Irish
and Miami at Yeatman's
Cove to work in pork and
liberation, gospel soaring
from the stage under
Southgate Bridge on
Sunday, Sawyer Park,
beneath the sycamore
and black oak and the
River Queen steaming
past the Wabash and
the Cumberland and
the Tennessee, the
Sultana, the shore fowl
and the catfish, the
elk and deer and
buffalo on the plains of
Hopewell and Adena,
Great Water feeding
the Great River and the
unfettered dreams of
Bakary and Jim by
the swift current swerving south.

Colonial Beach

Colonists flock to Colonial Beach
like terns on the Municipal Pier,
huddled close in August drizzle,
though not founded until 1892—
found long before by Powhatan,
sycamore shading coarse sand
from the grey sun behind mist
like oyster pirates in the heyday,
hiding from the Oyster Navy
while dredging the Potomac
in Oyster Wars, tongers raking
the lucrative beds for harvest,
Dancing Molly ducking police
until Berkley Muse met his doom.
Riverboats ceased steaming
from DC with revelers to resorts
when the automobile drove down
and the natives were conquered,
Playhouse booked, Riverview Inn
nevertheless flashing Vacancy,
crab pots showing like artifacts
outside the old Colonial museum,
wind now lashing the sycamores
like the terns on Municipal Pier
and the lapping Potomac waves.

Rappahannock

In the Tidewater
a breeze ripples
the red maple and
willow oak and
switchgrass—
hibiscus absorbs
the buzz of flies
and plish of
jumpfish that
catch them.
Crows caw the
heat but the
Rappahannock
is still, as the cliffs
where the tribes
fought John Smith
for their home, after
the tectonic shift
and meteor and
igneous rock, after
the river washed
over sediment
from Piedmont until
shale and quartz
became sand.
When the land was
bounty and beauty
and draught and
storm, laughter and
terror living like
heron and eagle
and bear and deer,
Topahanoke calm
on Opiscstumek
where the tide
ebbs and flows.
Where the Salvage
Mosco saved
Smith and crew

and changed his
name to Stranger.
Where the world
was sky and sun
beyond mountains,
and the honey
locust danced
and sang like the
heron and eagle
and Rappahannock breeze
rippling the maple and oak.

Pamunkey

A circle of cornmeal
for the Powhatan,
corn kernels for the
edge of the sea.
The Pamunkey ebbs
to the Great Water,
by Cinqueteck,
Werowocomoco,
the temple Uttamusack
where seven priests
attend the Chief,
praise the wetlands
and waterways,
oyster beds, beans
and squash,
cattapeuk and the
planting and fishing,
harvest and feasting,
sacrifice of blood
and deer—Mattaponi,
and Machicomoco
where tourists meet
in memory of
quioccosuks in
antlers and beads,
bearskins and shells
and Pamunkey
in scepters and pipes
who conjure the world.

Powhatan

Chief and
the tribes
and the river
are Powhatan
Bakary
learns as he
leans his craft
in the turn
to Richmond.
He knows the
plantations
on the banks
are chattel
farms where
his kind
are collared
and whipped
in the fields.
He pilots his
cargo past
the moorings
at market
toward
the rapids
where egrets
spear,
shad and
muskie reel,
mallard
and muskrat
plunge
in the marshes.
Wren and
warbler tell
Jim has freed
Sadie and
Mosco rowed
north with
his new wife.

What lives
beyond the
tide—the
rise and fall,
wars and
treaties,
slaves and
masters,
Shockoe Bottom
and Manchester
docks where
Africans arrive—
what peace
in the wide
channel
where runaways
hide in the
rushes,
longleaf shadow
the shore,
the Powhatan
becomes the
James and the
James opens
to the sea—

First Landing

At First Landing a pelican sings
to raptors in a rapture of discovery.
Of births and progeny, origins and
estuaries, voyages and villages.
Of the Great Water christened
Bahia de Santa Maria by Ajacán
to Chesapeake—Kecoughtan and
Paspihe millennia prior, land and
rivers named for the families.
Of oyster reefs white like Downes
by English through Indies to five
navigable—many rivers to cross—
faire and delightsome, sporting
panfish and sturgeon and scallop
by shallop past Nandsamund
and Weanock, Chickahaminy and
Chesepiooc, friendly and warrior.
Shores of pines and firs es pelican
chants, cormorants and cranes,
cypress swamps swimming with
snappers and snakes, boobies
and loons, sweetbay swaying sea
oats, fruitful valleyes of lusty soil,
fresh brookes and lush springs.
In this metaphor it's twenty myles
wide at the mouth hawk croons,
sole entry by sea, first is Powhatan,
three myles in breadth, plentie fish
by hooke, channell near to shore,
ground guilded with promise and
fortune as the Towne in his name.
Isles great and small of hickory and
oak, shrew and fox. Shoals and
rockes prevent further falcon chimes,
twelve houses on the hill below Falles
of glistering rundles and rapids by
hemp and flax and fields of gourd,
rich soil manured by colonists to
forts and farms, tobacco and slaves.

East for peace and wisdom, west for
rain and thunder, north the cleansing
wind, south source and end of life
osprey crows. Dolphins and porpoises
play in the current, crabs and clams
feed on beds of chalked sand like
the cliffs of Dover eagle roars, as
rivulets stream and memory soars,
the James flows into the Chesapeake,
the Chesapeake flows into the sea,
a pelican lifts at First Landing

and the river ends.

Clifford Bernier's The *Silent Art* won the Gival Press Poetry Award. He is also the author of *Dark Berries* and *Earth Suite,* each selected by the Montserrat Review as a Best Chapbook. A new book, *Ocean Suite,* was published in fall 2024, and his books *Wetlands* and *Chattel* were both published in spring 2025. He appears in *The Write Blend* poetry circle collection among other print and online journals and anthologies. In addition, Mr. Bernier appears on harmonica in the Portuguese *Accumulated Dust* world music series and is featured on the EP *Post-Columbian America.* He has been featured in readings in Los Angeles, Seattle, Chicago, Buffalo, Detroit, Philadelphia, Baltimore, and the Washington, DC area, including the Library of Congress, the Arts Club of Washington, George Washington University (where he is a member of the Washington Writer's Collection) and the Bethesda Writer's Center. He has been a reader for the Washington Prize and a judge for the National Endowment for the Arts' Poetry Out Loud recitation contest. From 2003-2008 he hosted the Poesis reading series in Arlington, Virginia and performed with the Jazzpoetry band at venues in and around Washington, DC. He has been nominated for two Pushcart Prizes and a Best of the Net Award. In May, 2025, Clifford lost his battle with cancer. He is survived by his wife and three adult children.

www.ingramcontent.com/pod-product-compliance
Lightning Source LLC
Chambersburg PA
CBHW030100170426
43197CB00010B/1603